THE
LOST ART
OF
Handwriting

WORKBOOK

PRACTICE SHEETS TO
IMPROVE YOUR PENMANSHIP

⟨ BRENNA JORDAN ⟩

Adams Media

New York   London   Toronto   Sydney   New Delhi

This workbook is dedicated to Jace, Jayva, and Jenaya.

Adams Media
An Imprint of Simon & Schuster, Inc.
100 Technology Center Drive
Stoughton, MA 02072

Copyright © 2021 by Simon & Schuster, Inc.

All rights reserved, including the right to reproduce this book or portions thereof in any form whatsoever. For information address Adams Media Subsidiary Rights Department, 1230 Avenue of the Americas, New York, NY 10020.

First Adams Media trade paperback edition January 2021

ADAMS MEDIA and colophon are trademarks of Simon & Schuster.

For information about special discounts for bulk purchases, please contact Simon & Schuster Special Sales at 1-866-506-1949 or business@simonandschuster.com.

The Simon & Schuster Speakers Bureau can bring authors to your live event. For more information or to book an event contact the Simon & Schuster Speakers Bureau at 1-866-248-3049 or visit our website at www.simonspeakers.com.

Interior design by Colleen Cunningham
Handwriting samples by Brenna Jordan

Manufactured in the United States of America

5 2023

Library of Congress Cataloging-in-Publication Data has been applied for.

ISBN 978-1-5072-1574-6

Many of the designations used by manufacturers and sellers to distinguish their products are claimed as trademarks. Where those designations appear in this book and Simon & Schuster, Inc., was aware of a trademark claim, the designations have been printed with initial capital letters.

Contains material adapted from the following title published by Adams Media, an Imprint of Simon & Schuster, Inc.: *The Lost Art of Handwriting* by Brenna Jordan, copyright © 2019, ISBN 978-1-5072-0936-3.

Contents

Part 3: Printing   131

Introduction

Handwriting is an art form like no other. Handwritten communication may seem antiquated, but with its intensely personal and beautiful nature, it is actually the perfect complement to the standardized fonts of our digital times. Your handwriting is different from everyone else's; it is a tangible reflection of your unique thoughts, emotions, and identity. This workbook is designed to take you on a joyful journey to gain solid principles and then develop your own personalized style. You can use the various letter styles you learn here to form words, phrases, and sentences—meaningful facets of language that have the power to shape and change lives.

Maybe you've already experienced some of the remarkable benefits of handwriting, such as the calm, creativity, and connection it invites. Or, maybe you're just beginning to delve into the craft. Either way, *The Lost Art of Handwriting Workbook* will help you improve your results. Don't let terms like *handwriting workbook* or *penmanship practice* evoke images of boring and repetitive schoolwork—the sophisticated lettering and inspiring quotes in this workbook make practice fun, which will keep you motivated. The short exercises can fit into any schedule, even if you only have a few minutes here and there, and the perforated pages make it easy to practice on a flat surface and take a few pages with you on the go. This book will teach you every lowercase and capital cursive and printed letter, as well as providing many interesting quotations to copy for longer practice. You'll even find ideas and inspiration for taking your writing to the next level with variations and flourishes. Plus, you can easily celebrate your successes by looking back over your progress as you make your way through the workbook.

Let *The Lost Art of Handwriting Workbook* help you cultivate a soothing hobby that produces gorgeous results. Your lovely handwritten works will bring a smile to anyone who reads them—yourself included!

PART 1

Getting Started

Before we delve into practicing specific letters, it's important to understand some key terms you'll see throughout the book. You'll then learn about the (very few) tools you'll need—a writing utensil and some paper. Whether you opt for a fancy ink pen or an old-fashioned Number 2 pencil, you'll find key features and functions to look for, and learn what to avoid. Finally, we'll go over ways you can make the most of this workbook—from finding time to practice to reviewing your work and making improvements.

Throughout your practice, always remember that your mindset is as essential to your practice as the tools you use. One key ingredient for your practice can be easily overlooked: a sense of fun and enjoyment. As you work on the technical aspects of good form and design, nurture an open, playful, and creative approach, and you will grow not just in handwriting finesse, but in self-discovery.

Helpful Terms

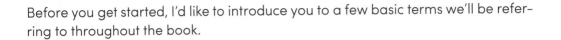

Before you get started, I'd like to introduce you to a few basic terms we'll be referring to throughout the book.

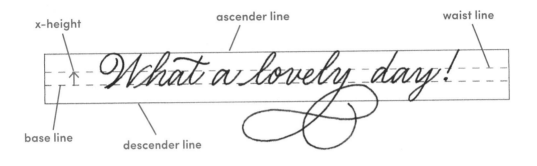

Guidelines are simply lines to help you write straight and keep your letters within a designated framework. The ones we will be using in the book are a little more detailed than basic notebook paper—they have additional lines showing where the tops and bottoms of your letters should land. You can use guidelines that are directly on your writing sheet, or place them behind a blank sheet that is transparent enough to see the lines through.

The **base line** is an important guideline for both uppercase and lowercase letters, as the letters will (in most cases) sit directly on this line. This will make your writing easier to read and also give it a neater appearance.

The **waist line** provides a boundary for the top of the x-height letters and a reference point for letters containing ascenders and descenders. For example, in the letters *d* and *g*, the rounded part of the letter will stop at the waist line, while the stem continues up or down.

The **ascender line** marks the spot where the tall stem in letters such as *b*, *d*, *f*, *k*, and *l* will touch. If the ascenders are too short, they can easily be confused with other letters.

The **descender line** marks the bottom of the letters *g*, *j*, *p*, *q*, and *y*, and the cursive *f*.

The **x-height** is the height of the lowercase *x*, *a*, *c*, *e*, *m*, *n*, and other letters that do not have ascenders or descenders.

The diagram shows the cursive phrase "What a lovely day!" with labels:
cross bar, counter, ascender, majuscule (uppercase letter), descender, flourish, minuscule (lowercase letter)

A **majuscule** is an uppercase, or capital, letter, and a **minuscule** is a lowercase letter.

An **ascender** is the portion of the lowercase letter that extends beyond the waist line, while a **descender** is the part of the letter that drops below the base line.

A **counter** is the enclosed space within a letter, such as in an *o*, *a*, or *d*.

Flourishing is the extra embellishment that you can incorporate into your handwriting, often at the ends of ascenders, descenders, and downstrokes, or on the **cross bars** (horizontal strokes) of letters such as *A*, *H*, *t*, and *f*.

●◆ practice tips

As your handwriting practice gains momentum, you might be surprised by how you will notice the hand lettering and typography around you with new interest. Carry a small notebook to jot down inspiration and ideas when they strike. Taking pictures of letters is one method of gathering ideas—for example, in signage or other typography that catches your eye. But I have found that it's even more helpful to take my own pencil to paper as often as possible to try improvising an alphabet for a fascinating letter I come across. I also have an alphabetical index file where I store the letters that I've written and don't want to forget. This way, when my ideas are at a low, I can turn to my collection for inspiration.

The Write Tools

The tools required for handwriting are simple items you most likely already have: pencils, pens, paper, and a few optional accessories. There are so many types of writing utensils, however, and the one you choose can make a huge difference in your enjoyment of practicing. Take your time experimenting—it's worth the investment to find a high-quality pen or pencil that fits comfortably in your hand and that you really like using.

Pencils

It can be confusing figuring out the grading system on pencils, so here's a brief overview. There are two grading scales referring to the graphite in pencils:

1. The first is numerical, with the number representing the hardness of the core. A lower number means that the core is softer and will produce darker lines.
2. The second grading system uses letters: *H* for hardness, *B* for blackness. *HB* is considered equivalent to an average Number 2 pencil, but different brands have their own regulations. A high number after the *H* means a harder core, while a high number following a *B* means a softer core.

Although they are blacker, the disadvantage to soft pencils is that they need to be sharpened more frequently. Hard pencils hold their point longer and will leave lighter, sharper lines. You may want to experiment with several brands and grades to find out what you like best. There are many more, but a few recommended pencils are **Blackwing**, **Staedtler Norica**, and **Staedtler** mechanical pencil.

Pens

You will also want to experiment to find a pen that you enjoy using when you practice handwriting. Make sure the pen feels comfortable in your hand and writes smoothly, without scratching, blotching, or smudging. Try a variety of types, and find what helps you lessen the pressure exerted through your fingers, hand, and wrist. After writing with a few different pens, take a look at the results. When you find a pen that makes your writing look fantastic, you will be more likely to keep up with your practice.

For pens, try **Uni-ball Vision**, **Signo**, or the **Pentel EnerGel**, or you can experiment with **Microns**, **Faber-Castell**, and **Paper Mate Liquid Expresso** pens. If you don't already own a fountain pen, try one as soon as you can! The right tool can be magical, and a good fountain pen takes handwriting to a whole new level.

I recommend the **LAMY Safari** fountain pen with a refillable ink reservoir. It's easy to refill and has nifty built-in contours for finger placement that make it comfortable to hold (try out several different brands in a pen store, if possible, before you decide which one to buy). Besides being really fun to write with, this pen enables me to write for long periods of time.

The **Pelikan Classic M205** is another fountain pen you might want to check out, as well as the **Scribe Sword**, the **Faber-Castell Ambition**, and the **Kaweco Classic Sport Guilloche 1930**. The **Platinum Preppy** is a disposable fountain pen that is easy on the budget, while many fountain pens use easy-to-replace cartridges, if you prefer that style.

⬤✛ fun facts

The first ballpoint pens in the US hit the market in 1945 as an alternative to fountain pens, which use nibs and cartridges for filling the ink. The public enthusiastically embraced the new pens when they were introduced, and quickly converted to the ball-bearing point, which dispensed the ink and didn't need refilling as often as a fountain pen. Later, disposable ballpoint pens replaced the refillable versions.

Paper

It's best to use **lined paper**, with detailed guidelines in place if you like the extra lines for keeping ascenders and descenders at a uniform height. I use an assortment of:

- Notebook or loose-leaf paper
- Rhodia pads (lined or dotted)
- Graph paper
- Moleskine or other lined journals

If you prefer **unlined paper**, use a weight that is transparent enough for you to put a sheet of guidelines behind. And remember to save a compilation of these practice sheets, so you will be able to look back and see your progress. You will be amazed at how much you can improve in a short time.

Optional Tools

A **slant board** allows you to work on a sloped surface if you prefer that over writing flat. Some people are also greatly helped by a **pencil grip** made with flexible plastic or rubber, which slips onto your writing utensil and makes it easier to keep a good hold if the pencil feels too narrow or slippery. If you find that your hand cramps easily or gets sweaty when writing, a pencil grip may be more comfortable and will enable you to write for a longer time.

How to Use This Book

This workbook is versatile, so make it work for your schedule and lifestyle.

Aim for regular, consistent practice, even if it has to be for shorter durations. That's preferable to long, sporadic writing sessions for a couple of reasons: Practically, your hand won't tire as easily. Also, you will have better luck solidifying what you've learned and applying it the next time you practice.

Each time you practice, give yourself time to warm up. It can simply be a few unpressured minutes to loosen up and get yourself in a relaxed and confident frame of mind. You might doodle some lines, shapes, or patterns, or scrawl words that you hear on the radio.

Take your time. After writing an exercise, take a few minutes to review what you've done before moving on to the next page. Notice what you like, star letters you are most happy with, take notes on what you might change. If desired, use lined, dotted, or grid paper to supplement your practice pages. Rather than stopping when you achieve stellar results with a letter or word, try to get at least three good ones in a row. That helps you practice "doing it right" and instill the movements firmly in your mind.

When you are feeling particularly critical about your work, set it aside for a while. It's easy to dismiss your work, seeing only the flaws. Your self-evaluation will probably get a lot more positive when you come back to a page with fresh eyes a few hours later.

Get feedback. Because you are working so closely with your letters, it can be difficult to analyze them. Having another set of eyes look at what you've written is invaluable for correcting issues like illegibility, crowding words too closely, not using enough margin, writing too big or too small, or other trouble spots you might not be aware of.

Find applications for what you're learning whenever you can. Keep this workbook and other practice materials handy, and use spare minutes for writing. Turn your practice into projects by making handmade gifts, writing lists by hand, designing your own return address stamp, or anything else that could combine a current hobby with handwriting.

As you work through the pages of this book, remember to look back on how far you've come. Note your progress and celebrate achievements before moving on to the next thing. Be gentle with yourself when you hit roadblocks or setbacks—they are also part of your growth process. By making handwriting an intentional part of your lifestyle, you will gain confidence, skill, and expertise in a craft that is both beautiful and beneficial.

PART 2

Cursive

The art of elegant cursive writing is an exciting endeavor! In this part, you'll work on techniques for individual letters as well as joining letters. Make sure you have a pen and paper that facilitate smooth writing—you'll want a smudgeproof pen that doesn't snag or bleed. Or, feel free to use a high-quality pencil, which is a favorite tool for many.

Try all the variations of each letter, especially if a particular letter is hard for you. You may find a variation that works better for you or looks more appealing to your eye. Uppercase letters are more challenging than the lowercase alphabet, so expect to move slower and perhaps allot more time for your practice sessions.

Once you gain proficiency in each letter of the alphabet, start adding some flair to your handwriting with extra loops and flourishes. Using double letters for impact is another way to show style and have fun with words. Thinking about the meaning of words and expressing a mood with how you write—for example, loose and flowing, or sharp and angular—is a gratifying way to experiment and add character to your writing.

One more bit of advice: Observe handwriting around you in daily life—on signs, book covers, product logos, etc. Note styles that you are drawn to or, conversely, find unsightly or difficult to decipher. Pay attention to script styles you enjoy, whether simple and austere or playful and full of loops. Put your observations to work when you practice. Think of your paper like a canvas for unlimited displays of color, design, and personality!

Lowercase Cursive Alphabet

Here are all the lowercase letters in one place for your reference. You can practice them all here, then again individually in the following pages.

a b c d e f g h i j k l m

n o p q r s t u v w x y z

Lowercase Letter Practice: *a*

Trace over the gray letters to practice, then write your own on the blank lines.

Lowercase Letter Practice: *b*

Trace over the gray letters to practice, then write your own on the blank lines.

Lowercase Letter Practice: c

Trace over the gray letters to practice, then write your own on the blank lines.

Lowercase Letter Practice: *d*

Trace over the gray letters to practice, then write your own on the blank lines.

Lowercase Letter Practice: e

Trace over the gray letters to practice, then write your own on the blank lines.

Lowercase Letter Practice: *f*

Trace over the gray letters to practice, then write your own on the blank lines.

Lowercase Letter Practice: *g*

Trace over the gray letters to practice, then write your own on the blank lines.

Lowercase Letter Practice: *h*

Trace over the gray letters to practice, then write your own on the blank lines.

Lowercase Letter Practice: *i*

Trace over the gray letters to practice, then write your own on the blank lines.

ii i   ii i   ii i

Lowercase Letter Practice: *j*

Trace over the gray letters to practice, then write your own on the blank lines.

Lowercase Letter Practice: *k*

Trace over the gray letters to practice, then write your own on the blank lines.

k k   k k   k k

Lowercase Letter Practice: *l*

Trace over the gray letters to practice, then write your own on the blank lines.

Lowercase Letter Practice: *m*

Trace over the gray letters to practice, then write your own on the blank lines.

Lowercase Letter Practice: *n*

Trace over the gray letters to practice, then write your own on the blank lines.

Lowercase Letter Practice: o

Trace over the gray letters to practice, then write your own on the blank lines.

Lowercase Letter Practice: *p*

Trace over the gray letters to practice, then write your own on the blank lines.

Lowercase Letter Practice: *q*

Trace over the gray letters to practice, then write your own on the blank lines.

Lowercase Letter Practice: *r*

Trace over the gray letters to practice, then write your own on the blank lines.

Lowercase Letter Practice: *s*

Trace over the gray letters to practice, then write your own on the blank lines.

Lowercase Letter Practice: *t*

Trace over the gray letters to practice, then write your own on the blank lines.

Lowercase Letter Practice: *u*

Trace over the gray letters to practice, then write your own on the blank lines.

Lowercase Letter Practice: *v*

Trace over the gray letters to practice, then write your own on the blank lines.

Lowercase Letter Practice: *w*

Trace over the gray letters to practice, then write your own on the blank lines.

Lowercase Letter Practice: x

Trace over the gray letters to practice, then write your own on the blank lines.

Lowercase Letter Practice: *y*

Trace over the gray letters to practice, then write your own on the blank lines.

Lowercase Letter Practice: z

Trace over the gray letters to practice, then write your own on the blank lines.

Uppercase Cursive Alphabet

Here are the uppercase letters for your reference. You can practice them all here, then again individually in the following pages.

A B C D E F G H I

J K L M N O P Q R

Uppercase Cursive Alphabet

Here are the uppercase letters for your reference. You can practice them all here, then again individually in the following pages.

S T U V W X Y Z

Uppercase Letter Practice: *A*

Trace over the gray letters to practice, then write your own on the blank lines.

Uppercase Letter Practice: *B*

Trace over the gray letters to practice, then write your own on the blank lines.

Uppercase Letter Practice: C

Trace over the gray letters to practice, then write your own on the blank lines.

Uppercase Letter Practice: *D*

Trace over the gray letters to practice, then write your own on the blank lines.

Uppercase Letter Practice: *E*

Trace over the gray letters to practice, then write your own on the blank lines.

Uppercase Letter Practice: *F*

Trace over the gray letters to practice, then write your own on the blank lines.

Uppercase Letter Practice: G

Trace over the gray letters to practice, then write your own on the blank lines.

Uppercase Letter Practice: *H*

Trace over the gray letters to practice, then write your own on the blank lines.

Uppercase Letter Practice: *I*

Trace over the gray letters to practice, then write your own on the blank lines.

Uppercase Letter Practice: J

Trace over the gray letters to practice, then write your own on the blank lines.

Uppercase Letter Practice: *K*

Trace over the gray letters to practice, then write your own on the blank lines.

Uppercase Letter Practice: *L*

Trace over the gray letters to practice, then write your own on the blank lines.

Uppercase Letter Practice: M

Trace over the gray letters to practice, then write your own on the blank lines.

Uppercase Letter Practice: *N*

Trace over the gray letters to practice, then write your own on the blank lines.

Uppercase Letter Practice: O

Trace over the gray letters to practice, then write your own on the blank lines.

Uppercase Letter Practice: *P*

Trace over the gray letters to practice, then write your own on the blank lines.

Uppercase Letter Practice: Q

Trace over the gray letters to practice, then write your own on the blank lines.

Uppercase Letter Practice: *R*

Trace over the gray letters to practice, then write your own on the blank lines.

Uppercase Letter Practice: *S*

Trace over the gray letters to practice, then write your own on the blank lines.

Uppercase Letter Practice: *T*

Trace over the gray letters to practice, then write your own on the blank lines.

Uppercase Letter Practice: *U*

Trace over the gray letters to practice, then write your own on the blank lines.

Uppercase Letter Practice: *V*

Trace over the gray letters to practice, then write your own on the blank lines.

Uppercase Letter Practice: *W*

Trace over the gray letters to practice, then write your own on the blank lines.

Uppercase Letter Practice: X

Trace over the gray letters to practice, then write your own on the blank lines.

Uppercase Letter Practice: Y

Trace over the gray letters to practice, then write your own on the blank lines.

Uppercase Letter Practice: Z

Trace over the gray letters to practice, then write your own on the blank lines.

Loop Variations

Try this subtle variation in the ascender loops derived from the graceful Copperplate style. This will help if your loops tend to be hard to control, too large, or irregularly slanted. The variation adds a slight pause and direction change: Instead of going directly from the base line to the ascender line, stop at the waist line, slightly shift your angle outward, and form your loop. You can also try eliminating loops entirely for a different look.

standard one step

e e l l f f h h k k b b

copperplate two steps

e e l l f f h h k k b b

or eliminate loops

l l h h k k k k b b

Loop Variation Quote Practice

Copy this quote using the loop variations shown or your own combination.

To be yourself,

just yourself,

is a great thing.

HENRY MILLER

Entrance and Exit Stroke Practice

Entrance and exit strokes in cursive letters are the lines leading into the letter or exiting after the letter is formed. The strokes can be written using two different orientations that can be described as underhand or overhand. Practice these underhand and overhand strokes, as isolated strokes and in letters, until they feel natural and fluid. It's beneficial to know both of them, as the variety adds interest to fine handwriting.

underhand stroke

overhand stroke

Underhand entrance/underhand exit

a a g g f f y y z z

Overhand entrance/overhand exit

g g y y f f z z

Underhand entrance/overhand exit

g g y y f f j j

Overhand entrance/underhand exit

g g h h a a k k

Entrance and Exit Stroke Practice

After you master the basic entrance and exit strokes, there's room for adding personality, as shown here. Practice this sentence using your own preferences.

You are enough

Other Lowercase Variations

Practice copying these lowercase letter variations—first in isolation, then try using them in the context of words to see how you can incorporate them in your own handwriting.

s s s u v w y

b f k o o p p r r r

Lowercase Quote Practice

Copy this quote. As you write, keep an eye on the slant of your letters to ensure the angle stays consistent on all four lines. Also watch for consistency in spacing between letters and words.

The journey of a thousand miles must begin with a single step

LAO TZU

Practice Lowercase with a Classic Pangram

Copy this pangram for extra practice.

the quick brown fox jumped over the lazy dog's back

Practice Lowercase with a Classic Pangram

Copy this pangram for extra practice.

the quick brown fox jumped over the lazy dog's back

Practice Lowercase Quotes with Flourishes

Experiment with extra flourishes by copying this quote.

Talent is only the starting point

IRVING BERLIN

Practice Lowercase Quotes with Flourishes

These quotes offer two levels of flourishes—a fancy version and a minimalist one. Practice copying them to see which works best for you.

creativity takes courage

HENRI MATISSE

arrange whatever pieces
come your way

VIRGINIA WOOLF

Upper- and Lowercase Cursive Practice

Try writing this quote, using what you've learned about variations in capital letters and loops.

Writing is thinking on paper.

WILLIAM ZINSSER

Upper- and Lowercase Cursive Practice

Practice writing this quote, which features a capital letter variation and combining lowercase letters.

One kind word can warm three winter months.

JAPANESE PROVERB

Practicing Capital *W*

Try copying this quote using a flourished *W*.

Work is love made visible.

Upper- and Lowercase Cursive Practice

Practice writing this quote to become more familiar with loop variations and flourishes on the letter *t*.

What we learn with pleasure, we never forget.

ALFRED MERCIER

Copperplate Capital Letters

For a variation on standard capital letters, copy these Copperplate capital letters on the blank lines.

A B C D E

F G H I J K

L M N O P

Copperplate Capital Letters

Practice the rest of the Copperplate capital letters on the blank lines.

Q R S T U

V W X Y Z

Spencerian Capital Letters

These Spencerian capital letters are a good choice when you want a very special capital letter. Try copying these letters.

Spencerian Capital Letters

Practice the rest of the Spencerian capital letters on the blank lines.

O P Q R S

T U V W X

Y Z

Capital A Variations

The following pages of uppercase variations written with words offer several styles of capital letters for you to practice in word form. Try these unique As.

Artistic   Always

Awesome   Anniversary

Capital A Variations

These *As* offer even more variety—including some swirls that give the word a whole new feel.

Action   Attitude

Angels   Around

Capital *B* Variations

The letter *B* allows for a range of curves and flourishes—try these in the space provided.

Brave Beautiful Believe

Benevolent Brilliant

Breathe Bloom

Capital *C* and *D* Variations

Copy these variations on the letters *C* and *D*.

Compassion Calm

Cupcakes Charisma

Decisive Dear Devoted

Capital *E* and *F* Variations

Practicing different capital letter variations in a word brings the letters to life so you can see how they "get along" with other letters. Try these *E*s and *F*s.

Energetic   Equality   Eager

Family   Fantastic   Friend

Fforever

Capital *G* and *H* Variations

Copy these variations on the letters *G* and *H*.

Good Grateful

Grace Gorgeous

Happy Humor Healthy

Capital *I* and *J* Variations

The double loops on some of these *I*s and *J*s add some extra flair. Try to copy these *I* and *J* variations.

Invincible Ideal Inky

Joyous Jolly

Capital *K*, *L*, and *M* Variations

Copy these variations on the letters *K*, *L*, and *M*.

Kindness   Knowledge

Laughter   Light   Love

Magical   Mindful

Capital *N*, *O*, and *P* Variations

Copy these variations on the letters *N*, *O*, and *P*.

Nourish   Natural

Open   Organized   Patient

Peaceful   Pristine

Capital *Q* and *R* Variations

You can take the letter *Q* in two different directions—one playing off the printed *Q*, and the other the traditional cursive *Q*. Try these *Q*s and *R*s.

Quiet Quintessential

Relaxed Rested Radiant

Capital *S* and *T* Variations

Copy these variations on the letters *S* and *T*.

Simple Significant Safe

Trust Travel Timeless

Capital *W*, *Y*, and *Z* Variations

Copy these variations on the letters *W*, *Y*, and *Z* (*U*, *V*, and *X* are not included because those letters aren't as common).

Winter Wisdom Write

Youthful Yesterday Yoga

Zestful Zany Zephyr

Quote Practice

Copy the quote, practicing these simple ways you can dress up your writing. When you add flourishes, remember that you want to create a design that doesn't distract from the words but rather enhances the message.

Leave the road,
Take the trails.

PYTHAGORAS

Leave the road,
Take the trails.

Leave the road
Take the trails.

Quote Practice

Start by copying the two examples. You can see how simple design additions can dramatically change the overall look and feel of a piece of writing. If you're ready for additional practice, create your own design, using the flourishing opportunities on the ascenders, descenders, and cross bars.

Let your conversation be always full of grace

Let your conversation be always full of grace

Letter Joins with *a*

Admirable handwriting is marked by proper letter joins. With most letter combinations, joining the letters flows fairly naturally, but there are a few difficult letter joins that require extra thought and attention. We'll start with the vowels. Try these *a*-based letter joins.

ab   *ac*   *ad*

ae   *af*   *ag*

ah   *ai*   *aj*

ak   *al*   *am*

an   *ao*   *ap*

aq   *ar*   *as*

at   *au*   *av*

aw   *ax*   *ay*

az

Letter Joins with *a*: Word Practice

Copy these phrases, focusing on the *a* joins.

an apple a day

as happy as a clam

Letter Joins with e

Twenty-two of the twenty-six letters have an exit stroke that starts at the base line, such as *e*. Because of this opportune placement, most of the letters in the alphabet lead into the next letter fairly easily. Try these *e*-based letter joins.

ea   *eb*   *ec*

ed   *ef*   *eg*

eh   *ei*   *ej*

ek   *el*   *em*

en   *eo*   *ep*

eq   *er*   *es*

et   *eu*   *ev*

ew   *ex*   *ey*

ez   *ee*   *ee*

Letter Joins with e: Word Practice

Copy this phrase, focusing on the *e* joins.

educate the heart

Letter Joins with *i*

Copy these *i*-based letter joins.

ia   ib   ic

id   ie   if

ig   ih   ij

ik   il   im

in   io   ip

iq   ir   is

it   iu   iv

iw   ix   iy   iz

Letter Joins with *i*: Word Practice

Copy this sentence, focusing on the *i* joins.

What seems to us as bitter trials are often blessings in disguise.

OSCAR WILDE

Letter Joins with *o*

Copy these *o*-based letter joins.

oa   ob   oc
od   oe   of
og   oh   oi
oj   ok   ol
om   on   op
oq   or   os
ot   ou   ov
ow   ox   oy   oz

Letter Joins with *o*: Word Practice

Copy this sentence, focusing on the *o* joins.

I can live for two months on a good compliment.

Letter Joins with *u*

Copy these *u*-based letter joins.

ua   ub   uc

ud   ue   uf

ug   uh   ui

uj   uk   ul

um   un   uo

up   uq   ur

us   ut   uv

uw   ux   uy   uz

Letter Joins with *u*: Word Practice

Copy this sentence, focusing on the *u* joins.

the purpose of art is
washing the dust of
daily life off our souls.

Letter Joins with *p*

Now let's move on to some common consonants. Copy these *p*-based letter joins.

pa   *pb*   *pc*

pd   *pe*   *pf*

pg   *ph*   *pi*

pj   *pk*   *pl*

pm   *pn*   *po*

pp   *pq*   *pr*

ps   *pt*   *pu*

pv   *pw*   *px*

py   *pz*

Letter Joins with *p*: Word Practice

Copy this sentence, focusing on the *p* joins.

please pass the peas

Letter Joins with *r*

Copy these *r*-based letter joins.

ra   *rb*   *rc*

rd   *re*   *rf*

rg   *rh*   *ri*

rj   *rk*   *rl*

rm   *rn*   *ro*

rp   *rq*   *rr*

rs   *rt*   *ru*

rv   *rw*   *rx*

ry   *rz*

Letter Joins with *r*: Word Practice

Copy this sentence, focusing on the *r* joins.

perfect love drives out fear

JOHN THE APOSTLE

Letter Joins with *t*

Copy these *t*-based letter joins.

ta   *tb*   *tc*

td   *te*   *tf*

tg   *th*   *ti*

tj   *tk*   *tl*

tm   *tn*   *to*

tp   *tq*   *tr*

ts   *tu*   *tv*

tw   *tx*   *ty*   *tz*

Letter Joins with *t*: Word Practice

You'll see that the angle of the line connecting letters will change based on what type of join it is. Two parallel letters (like *ts* and *ls*) will require a differently angled join than a straight letter with a round letter (*t* and *o*, for example) or two round letters (*a* and *d*). Copy this sentence, focusing on the *t* joins.

Never give up, for that is just the place and time that the tide will turn!

HARRIET BEECHER STOWE

Letter Joins with *b*

The letters *b*, *o*, *v*, and *w* are the four letters that deviate from the norm. These letters have an exit stroke at the waist line—a small swooping stroke that looks like the smile on a smiley face. In spite of its happy shape, this exit stroke sometimes makes it difficult to connect with other letters of the alphabet. The key is to make this line distinct enough to maintain legibility as it melds with the next letter. For example, take a look at the *b-e* combination here. The exit stroke of the *b* becomes part of the loop of the *e*, but there is enough space between the two to distinguish the two letters. In the *b-r* combo, the angle of the exit stroke curves upward to allow for the first stroke of the *r*.

ba be bi bl bo br bu

ba ba   be be

bi bi   bo bo

br br   bl bl

Letter Joins with *o*, *v*, and *w*

The *o–r* and *o–s* combinations are also typically awkward. For legibility, both the *r* and the *s* work best starting at the base line, but here they are forced to start at the waist line. Try dropping the exit stroke of the *o* a bit (just enough to not look like an *a*) to allow room for an exaggerated entrance into the *r* and the *s*. The *w–r* combo is similar.

oa oe oi or os ou ow ox

oe   *oe*   *oi*   *oi*

or   *or*   *os*   *os*

ow   *ow*   *ox*   *ox*

va ve vo vy wr wo wh wi

va   *va*   *vy*   *vy*

wr   *wr*   *wo*   *wo*

wh   *wh*   *wi*   *wi*

Letters with Descender-to-Ascender Joins

Another letter connection to watch for is the descender-to-ascender join. For some of these letter pairs, your pen needs to travel from the descender line to the ascender line in one long movement, with the goal of keeping this stroke smooth and steady enough to blend in with the rest of the word. The most common examples of this join are found in the *g–h*, *g–l*, and *y–l* letter combinations.

Letters with Tricky Joins: Word Practice

Practice writing these phrases with various tricky letter joins.

sursum corda

hors d'oeuvres

you've got rhythm

Fun Ways to Practice: Writing Names

It can be monotonous practicing lines of the same letter over and over. To make it more interesting, go through the alphabet using the names of people or places, such as Australia, Brazil, Canada...Zimbabwe! This way you will be practicing both uppercase and lowercase letters and also working on spacing and joining letters. Try these names to inspire you.

Aria Beth Carl Dave

Evan Fern Gina Herb

Iris Jace Kate Levi

Fun Ways to Practice: Writing Names

Continue practicing with these names.

Mary Nina Otto Pavo

Quin Reed Seth Tara

Vera Wade Yana Zoey

Double Letters: Identical Twins

You can write double letters in a traditional way: Make those two letters look uniform in size and shape. If legibility and formality are of utmost consideration, this choice might be the natural way to go.

happiness can exist only in acceptance.

GEORGE ORWELL

Double Letters: Fraternal Twins

Here's another way to approach double letters—by writing the second letter a bit smaller than the first. (You could also try contrasting their heights, loops, hills, or flourishes so they share similarities but march to the beat of their own drummer.) Copy this quote to practice using varied second letter size.

happiness lies in the joy of achievement and the thrill of creative effort.

FRANKLIN D. ROOSEVELT

Ascender and Descender Flourishes

Ascenders and descenders offer perfect opportunities to add some embellishment. Capitals are conducive to flourishing, as well as letters with cross bars. The beginnings and ends of words also work well, and these flourishes are especially helpful when you are working to create balance in a word.

Ascender and Descender Flourishes

Try mirroring these flourishes or create your own.

H and *F* Flourishes

Try to copy this simple quote about friendship. In this example, the ascender and descender flourishes are reserved for the outside of the piece, rather than the middle lines, for visual clarity.

There is nothing on this earth more to be prized than true friendship.

Quote Practice

Copy the following quote, varying your flourish style. If you need more space, continue practicing on the blank pages at the back of the book.

Always remember
to forget
the friends that
proved untrue,
But never forget
to remember
those that have
stuck by you.

Quote Practice

Copy this flourished quote. This quote works perfectly for achieving balance, since the top line contains an ascender letter, and the bottom line has a descender. For extra practice, try as many of the *k* ascender and *p* descender flourishes as you'd like. If you need more space, continue practicing on the blank pages at the back of the book.

Not taking things personally is a superpower!

JAMES CLEAR

Quote Practice

Copy this quote slowly to help develop a smooth rhythm as you write. When you're finished, take a minute to evaluate the consistency in your slant and spacing. Does the angle stay the same on each line? Look over your spacing between letters and words to notice any inconsistencies there. (Tip: It helps to turn the page upside down!) This quote contains a lot of loop letters. Check to see if you maintained a similar size for these counters (the space within the loops) and consistently rounded turns, rather than sharp, abrupt ones. If you need more space, continue practicing on the blank pages at the back of the book.

If you think you can't do something, or if you are afraid to do something, that's exactly when you should do it.

PART 3

Printing

While cursive is reminiscent of a graceful dance, printing is more of a triumphal march. Since the letters stand alone and consist of more straight lines and lifting of your writing utensil, printing practice requires a slightly different mentality and use of fine motor skills. Having a good grasp of both print and cursive will give you flexibility and more varied opportunities for creative expression.

Understanding and practicing the right proportions of the Roman Skeleton capitals will help every style of your writing improve! Spend time etching these family groups of the Roman caps in your memory, and you will be able to see progress almost immediately in legibility, neatness, and consistency. It's ideal to practice using grid paper, so you can check your proportions and develop a good eye for accuracy.

Once you've learned the basics of the Roman capitals, there's no limit to variations of print. You can stretch letters wider or draw them tall and narrow. You can use cross bars to vary the personality of print by extending them, crossing them low or high, or using an undulating line instead of a straight one. Just adding serifs (those accents at the edges of letters) to a sans serif alphabet will give your print an entirely different vibe.

After you've mastered a handful of print styles, it's fun to use a mix of print and cursive in your creative projects such as addressing envelopes, designing layouts for quotes, making gift tags, and bullet journaling.

Mastering Roman Capitals

The fact that Roman capitals are the foundation for our alphabet speaks of their enduring and powerful quality. In fact, their impressive design, dating back well over two thousand years, provides a window into the power and majesty of the ancient Roman Empire. At that time in history, the letters were brush-drawn and then cut in stone with a chisel and mallet. A few of the most famous inscriptions of Roman capitals can be seen on such landmarks as Trajan's Column, the Arch of Titus, and the Roman Pantheon.

Roman capitals are clean and basic, but it takes a lot of skill to write them well. Therefore, don't expect to master them in a short amount of time. Be patient with yourself and try not to rush your practice. Here are a few things to keep in mind as you practice Roman capitals:

Respect the proportions. Learning the proportions of each family group will give you an underlying foundation for writing that will revolutionize your understanding of letters and your ability to produce stellar ones.

Look for straight lines and circles. Identifying these key parts of each letter will help you break it down into smaller chunks as you learn.

Connect the dots. When you construct your own letters, draw a few dots in key spots first, and then connect them. This will help take the guesswork out of where the strokes should start and end, and give you the guidance needed to make accurate forms. Use the dots until you feel comfortable forming the letters without them.

Observe Roman capitals wherever you go. They are on wine bottles, signs, posters, menus, magazines, book covers, and logos, to name a few. Note the versatility they offer and the respect they command.

Use graph paper whenever possible for practicing. Until you have a good handle on the proportions and can maintain them consistently, the grid lines will help you keep your letters straight and even.

Because of the precision and discipline required to learn Roman capitals, your work with them will also help every other style of writing become easier to learn. And for an added bonus, this will prepare you to take the next step to learn broad-edged or brush-lettered Romans with their thick and thin strokes and elegant serifs. In the meantime, the monoline Romans we practice here, also called Skeleton Roman letters, are a useful and beautiful addition to your handwriting repertoire.

Uppercase Roman Alphabet

Here are all the uppercase Roman letters in one place for your reference. You can practice them all here, then again individually in the following pages.

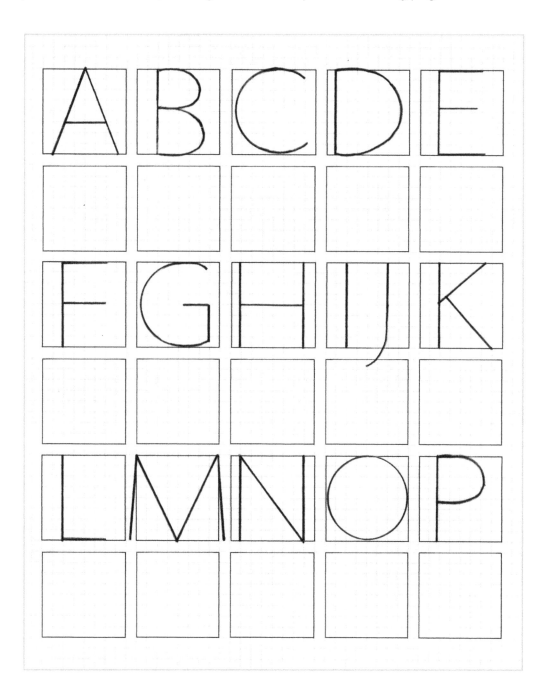

Uppercase Roman Alphabet

Here are all the uppercase Roman letters in one place for your reference. You can practice them all here, then again individually in the following pages.

Uppercase Letter Practice: *A* and *B*

The *A* is an upside-down *V* with a cross bar placed one grid section below the center of the square. This creates visual balance. The bottom portion of the *B* extends a little beyond the first section. Trace the example letter, then practice on your own in the blank boxes provided.

Uppercase Letter Practice: *C* and *D*

Trace the example letter, then practice on your own in the blank boxes provided.

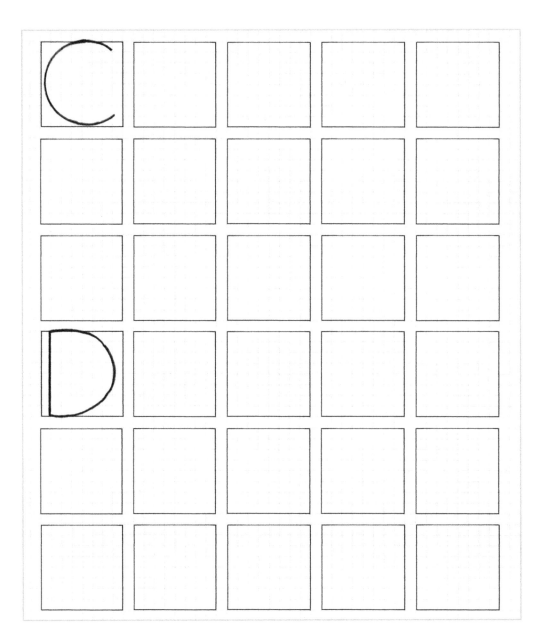

Uppercase Letter Practice: *E* and *F*

In the *E*, the bottom line extends out slightly beyond the top line to keep the *E* from looking like it may topple over. The middle cross bar of the *E* is a bit above the center line. In the *F*, the middle cross bar is exactly centered. Trace the example letter, then practice on your own in the blank boxes provided.

Uppercase Letter Practice: *G* and *H*

Trace the example letter, then practice on your own in the blank boxes provided.

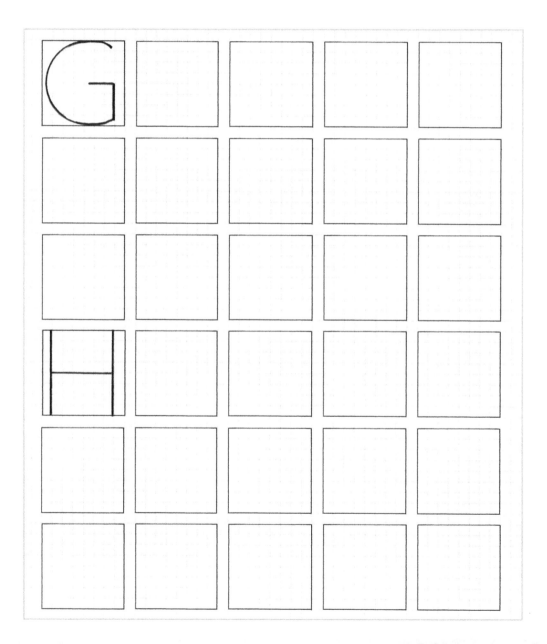

Uppercase Letter Practice: *I* and *J*

Trace the example letter, then practice on your own in the blank boxes provided.

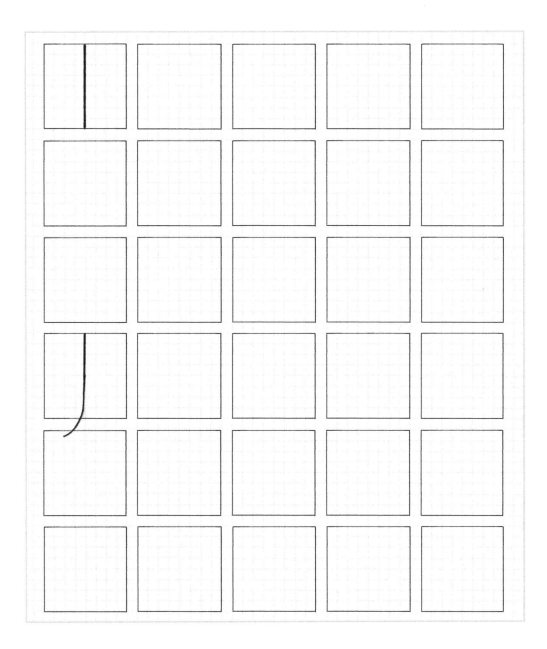

Uppercase Letter Practice: *K* and *L*

The bottom diagonal of the *K* kicks out farther than the top arm to keep the letter from looking imbalanced and top heavy. Trace the example letter, then practice on your own in the blank boxes provided.

Uppercase Letter Practice: *M* and *N*

The two outer lines of the *M* extend just beyond the grid square on each side. The *N* is similar to the *H* with two identical sides to the rectangular shape. The difference is that instead of the middle cross bar of the *H*, the *N* has a diagonal line starting at the top left and moving down to the bottom right-hand corner of the letter. Trace the example letter, then practice on your own in the blank boxes provided.

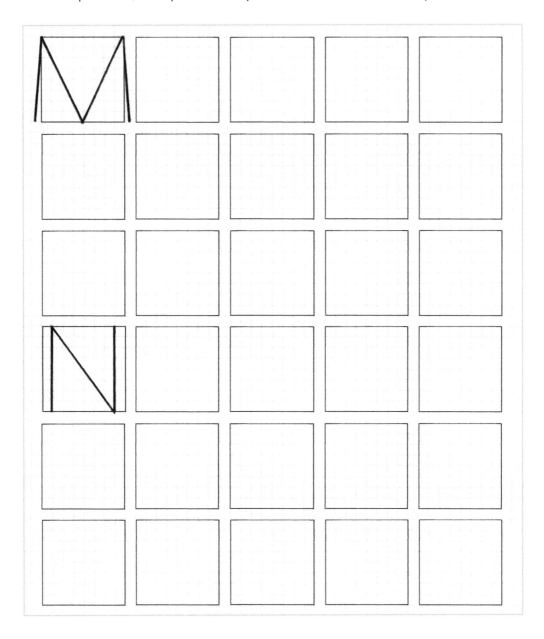

Uppercase Letter Practice: *O* and *P*

Trace the example letter, then practice on your own in the blank boxes provided.

Uppercase Letter Practice: Q and R

The foot of the R kicks out a bit to support the top half of the letter. Trace the example letter, then practice on your own in the blank boxes provided.

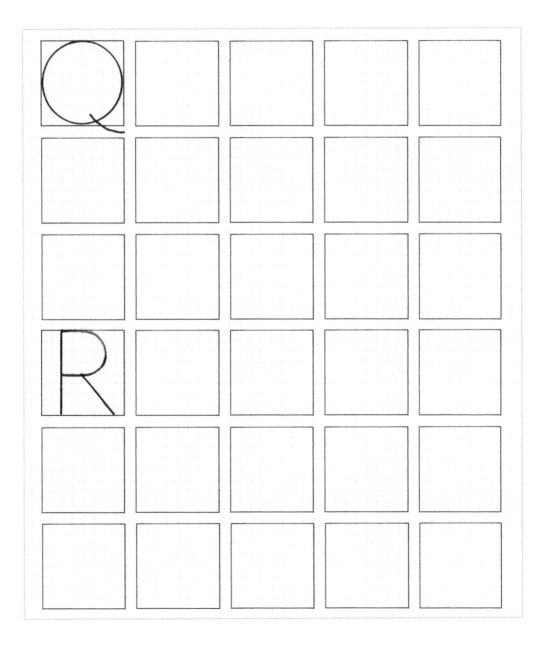

Uppercase Letter Practice: *S* and *T*

The bottom portion of the *S* extends a little beyond the top section. Trace the example letter, then practice on your own in the blank boxes provided.

Uppercase Letter Practice: *U* and *V*

Trace the example letter, then practice on your own in the blank boxes provided.

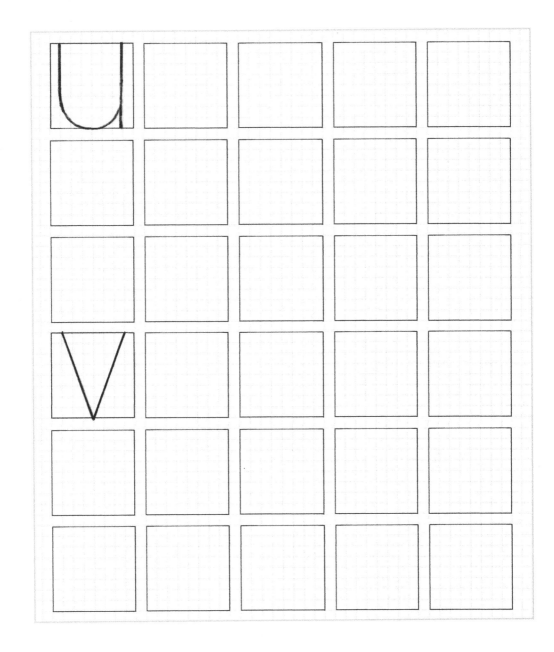

Uppercase Letter Practice: *W* and *X*

The *W* is not an upside-down *M*. The proportions are notably different, with the outer lines of the *W* extending out. If you turn the *X* upside down, you will see that the bottom part is larger than the top. To create this balance, move the top lines of the *X* in a little bit. This will cause the *X* to cross slightly above the middle line. Trace the example letter, then practice on your own in the blank boxes provided.

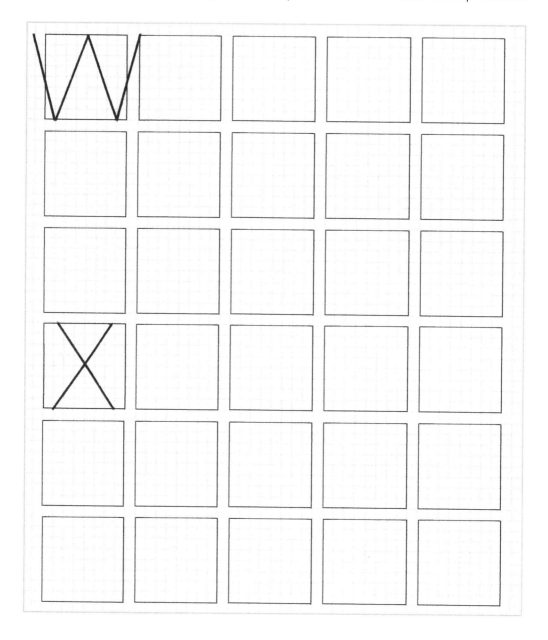

Uppercase Letter Practice: Y

The two arms of the Y meet just above the center point of the square, where the bottom stem of the Y joins them. This positioning helps create a stable base for the top of the Y. Trace the example letter, then practice on your own in the blank boxes provided.

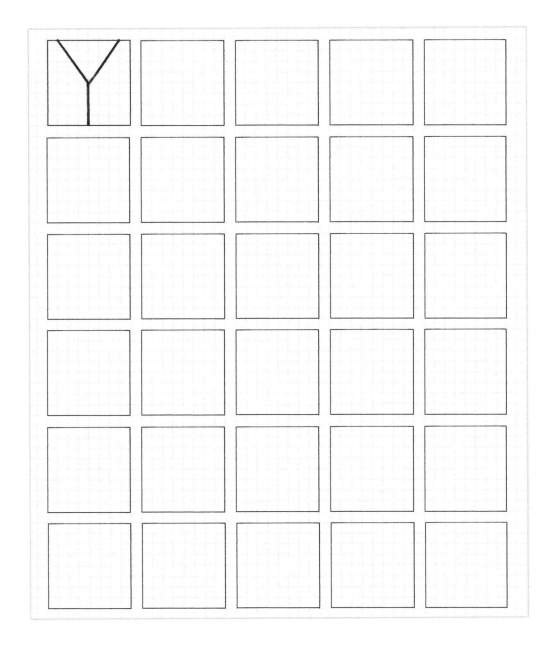

Uppercase Letter Practice: Z

The bottom line of the Z is just slightly longer than the top line, again for balance and visual appeal. Trace the example letter, then practice on your own in the blank boxes provided.

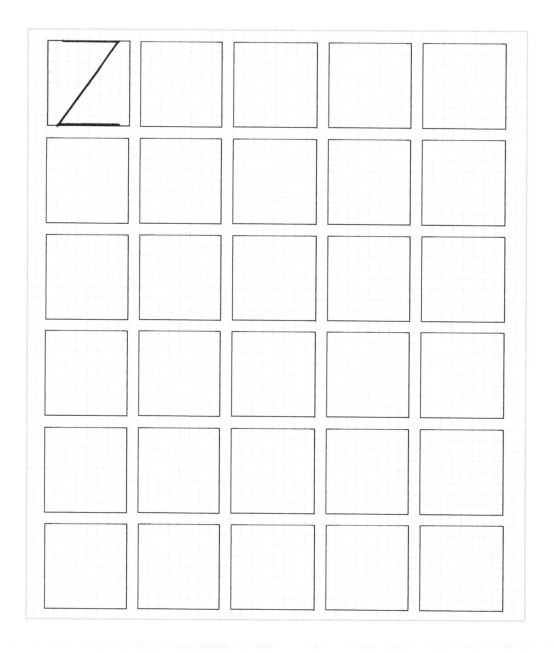

Roman Capital Letter Spacing

When spacing Roman capitals, you will need to consider what letter comes next in order to decide how much space to leave. Two round sides need to be placed closer together than a rounded side next to a straight edge. And two straight edges will need more space between them than either of the previous two examples. You can also be creative in your use of cross bars to make Roman letters look more interesting. Copy this quote to practice spacing with Roman letters.

THE MIND
WAS BUILT FOR
MIGHTY FREIGHT

EMILY DICKINSON

Roman Capital Letter Spacing

Copy this word to practice spacing with Roman letters.

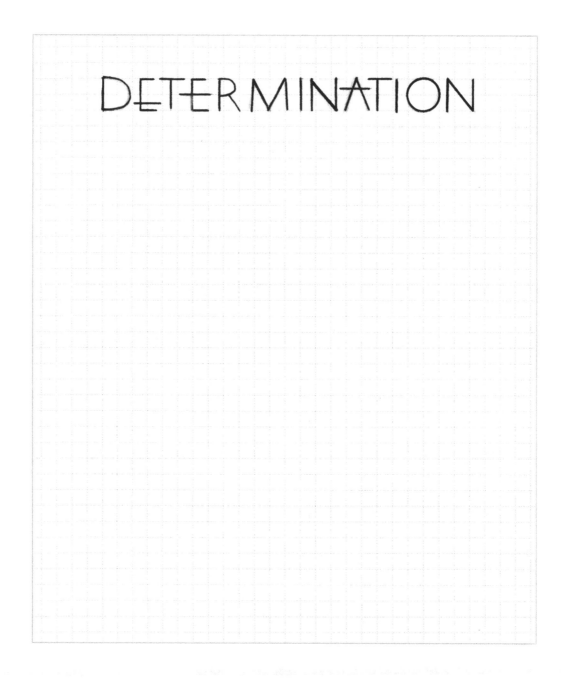

DETERMINATION

Roman Letter Spacing with Double Letters

Double letters provide an opportunity to add interesting visual elements, such as overlapping letters, making them touch, or using unique cross bars. Copy this quote to practice.

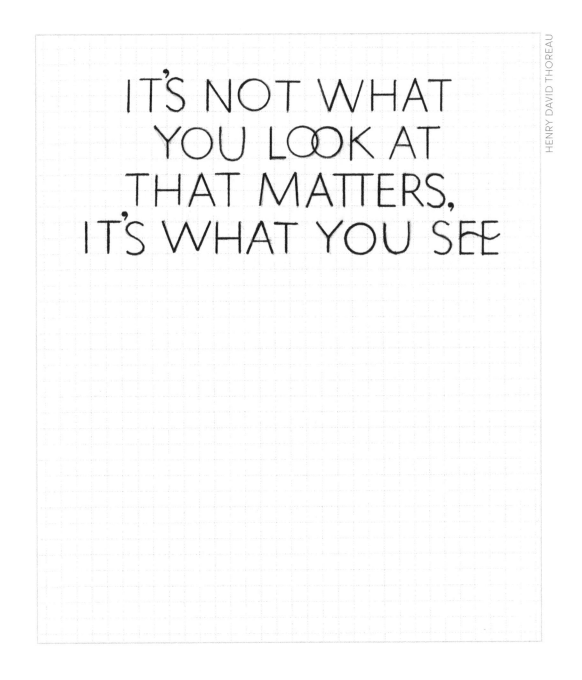

IT'S NOT WHAT YOU LOOK AT THAT MATTERS, IT'S WHAT YOU SEE

HENRY DAVID THOREAU

Roman Letter Spacing with Double Letters

Copy the quote again, but this time design your own double letter flourishes.

Roman Letter Spacing with Italic Print

Copy this quote to practice Roman letters with italic print mixed in for flair and effect.

The secret of
PATIENCE
is to do something else
in the meantime.

Roman Letter Spacing with Italic Print

Copy the quote again, but this time interpret the design in your own way.

Quote Practice

Here's a chance to have fun with all-capital print in a compact design. Observe the effects of balanced flourishing that flows into letter strokes, the creative use of cross bars, and how the spacing, layout, and flourishing all contribute to the meaning of the quote.

EVERY
GREAT
DREAM
BEGINS
WITH A
DREAMER

HARRIET TUBMAN

Quote Practice

Copy this rhythmic quote with four lines each of script and print. This will help the transition from cursive to print become more natural. You can end with a simple flourish on the cross bar of the *F*, or take your practice a step further and add any other embellishments around the quote to illustrate the garden theme. If you need more space, continue practicing on the blank pages at the back of the book.

Kind hearts are the

GARDENS,

kind thoughts are the

ROOTS.

Kind words are the

BLOSSOMS,

kind deeds are the

FRUITS.

HENRY WADSWORTH LONGFELLOW

Lowercase Italic Alphabet

Italic print is slightly slanted, highly legible, simple to execute, and pleasing to the eye. Here is the full lowercase alphabet for your reference. We'll practice each letter on the pages ahead.

a b c d e f g h i j k l m

n o p q r s t u v w x y z

Lowercase Italic Alphabet

Continue to practice copying these lowercase italic letters.

a b c d e f g h i j k l m

n o p q r s t u v w x y z

Lowercase Italic Letters: *a* and *b*

Practice tracing the letters on the gray versions. Remember to make the spine of the letter straight, and add the curve toward the very bottom of the line.

a a a   a a   a a

b b b   b b   b b

Lowercase Italic Letters: c and d

Practice tracing the letters on the gray versions. Remember to make the spine of the letter straight, and add the curve toward the very bottom of the line.

c c c   c c   c c

d d d   d d   d d

Lowercase Italic Letters: *e* and *f*

Note that the rounded letters are more oval than circular. Practice tracing the letters on the gray versions, then make your own letters on the blank lines provided.

e e e   e e   e e

f f f   f f   f f

Lowercase Italic Letters: *g* and *h*

Practice tracing the letters on the gray versions, then make your own letters on the blank lines provided.

g g g   g g   g g

h h h   h h   h h

Lowercase Italic Letters: *i*, *j*, and *k*

Practice tracing the letters on the gray versions, then make your own letters on the blank lines provided.

i *i* *i*　　*i* *i*　　*i* *i*

j *j* *j*　　*j* *j*　　*j* *j*

k *k* *k*　　*k* *k*　　*k* *k*

Lowercase Italic Letters: *l*, *m*, and *n*

Practice tracing the letters on the gray versions, then make your own letters on the blank lines provided.

l l l   l l   l l

m m m   m m   m m

n n n   n n   n n

Lowercase Italic Letters: *o, p,* and *q*

Practice tracing the letters on the gray versions, then make your own letters on the blank lines provided.

o o o   o o   o o

p p p   p p   p p

q q q   q q   q q

Lowercase Italic Letters: *r, s,* and *t*

Practice tracing the letters on the gray versions, then make your own letters on the blank lines provided.

r r r   r r   r r

s s s   s s   s s

t t t   t t   t t

Lowercase Italic Letters: *u* and *v*

Practice tracing the letters on the gray versions, then make your own letters on the blank lines provided.

u u u   u u   u u

v v v   v v   v v

Lowercase Italic Letters: *w, x, y,* and *z*

Practice tracing the letters on the gray versions, then make your own letters on the blank lines provided.

w w w   w w   w w

x x x   x x   x x

y y y   y y   y y

z z z   z z   z z

Practicing Lowercase Italic Letters in Quotes

Copy this short quote to practice lowercase italic letters.

work is love
made visible

KAHLIL GIBRAN

Practicing Lowercase Italic Letters in Quotes

Copy this short quote to practice lowercase italic letters.

*well done is
better than well said*

BENJAMIN FRANKLIN

Uppercase Italic Alphabet

Uppercase italic letters use many of the same strokes and angles as the lowercase letters. Here is the full uppercase alphabet for your reference. We'll practice each letter on the pages ahead.

A B C D E F
G H I J K L
M N O P
Q R S T U V
W X Y Z

Uppercase Italic Alphabet

Continue to practice copying these uppercase italic letters.

A B C D E F
G H I J K L
M N O P
Q R S T U V
W X Y Z

Uppercase Italic Letters: *A, B,* and *C*

Practice tracing the letters on the gray versions, then make your own letters on the blank lines provided. *Ductus,* the Latin word for "leading," shows the sequence and direction of the strokes that make up a letter.

Uppercase Italic Letters: *D, E,* and *F*

Practice tracing the letters on the gray versions, then make your own letters on the blank lines provided.

D D D   D D

E E E   E E

F F F   F F

Uppercase Italic Letters: *G, H,* and *I*

Practice tracing the letters on the gray versions, then make your own letters on the blank lines provided.

Uppercase Italic Letters: *J, K,* and *L*

Practice tracing the letters on the gray versions, then make your own letters on the blank lines provided.

Uppercase Italic Letters: *M, N,* and *O*

Practice tracing the letters on the gray versions, then make your own letters on the blank lines provided.

Uppercase Italic Letters: *P*, *Q*, and *R*

Practice tracing the letters on the gray versions, then make your own letters on the blank lines provided.

Uppercase Italic Letters: *S, T, U,* and *V*

Practice tracing the letters on the gray versions, then make your own letters on the blank lines provided.

Uppercase Italic Letters: *W, X, Y,* and *Z*

Practice tracing the letters on the gray versions, then make your own letters on the blank lines provided.

Numbers and Punctuation

The number samples on this and the following page work for both printing or cursive. When using numbers with text, choose styles that match or complement one another. It helps to write all ten numbers to discover your favorite ones. Copy these number and punctuation styles on the blank lines provided.

1234567890 !?&

1234567890!?&

Numbers and Punctuation

These styles merely scratch the surface, so if you'd like more practice, try making your own set of numbers. Copy these number and punctuation styles on the blank lines provided.

1234567890 !?&

1234567890!?&

1234567890

Quote Practice

Utilizing both script and print is an ideal way to add interest to your writing. Think about what words you'd like to emphasize, and experiment until you come up with a balanced design. Copy this design, and for an extra challenge, choose your own short quote (ten words or fewer) and create a similar design using both cursive and print.

Live life as though EVERYTHING *is rigged in your favor*

Quote Practice

Copy the quote. Most of the quote is in typewriter print, but the two action words will give you a chance to practice modern script. For an extra challenge, reverse the script and print! Start with a legible cursive style, and write the action words in all caps.

True belonging
doesn't require you to
Change who you are;
it requires you to
Be who you are.

BRENÉ BROWN

Quote Practice

Copy this quote using the sans serif print style. Try your hand at embellishing print with the simple flourish off the *y*. If you'd like an extra challenge, create more flourishing off the ascenders and cross bars on the first line of text.

What other people
think of me is
none of my business.

ELEANOR ROOSEVELT

Quote Practice

Short quotes are great for practicing composition! First, write out the quote, assessing the length and importance of the words, and the meaning and mood of the quote. In this short poem excerpt, I chose to emphasize the words *feeling* and *final*, so I started them with capital letters. For balanced flourishing, the ascender of the *l* and a disconnected flourish on the bottom frame the quote. The shorter words in typewriter print are a contrast to the ornamental script. Practice copying this quote, then choose your own four- or five-word saying to design a similar composition using script and print to portray the meaning.

no feeling is final

RAINER MARIA RILKE

No *Feeling* is *Final*

Quote Practice

Try copying this quote using different cursive or print styles.

At the point of the pen is the focus of the mind

JAMES LENDALL BASFORD

Quote Practice

Copy this quote, focusing on unique crosses on the *ts*.

Fill your paper with the breathings of your heart

WILLIAM WORDSWORTH

Quote Practice

How you write a word can give clues to the meaning of the word. Here, the key word *humor* takes on a personality of its own. You can use this technique in your handwriting when you want a word to play a lead role on stage and attract more attention than the "supporting actors." As you write this quote, concentrate on relaxing your hand. This will help your flourishes look even and smooth, and give your penmanship a gentle, wavelike ebb and flow.

MARK TWAIN

Humor is the spiciest condiment in the feast of existence.

ABOUT THE ARTIST

"I know nothing in the world that has as much power as a word. Sometimes I write one, and I look at it, until it begins to shine."
—EMILY DICKINSON

Brenna Jordan was introduced to the art of calligraphy in sixth grade when she received a pen set for Christmas. Completely mesmerized, she began studying books on lettering and quickly found that it was the perfect match for her interest in words and quotes. Eventually her lifelong hobby evolved into a business, Calligraphy by Brenna.

She enjoys working on a wide variety of projects for clients (especially writing on more unusual surfaces like stones, pressed leaves, birch bark, and walls) and sharing her love for lettering with students as well as her online community. She's especially enthusiastic about flourishing, and how it transforms language into something extraordinary and expressive.

Brenna is a member of IAMPETH (the International Association of Master Penmen, Engrossers, and Teachers of Handwriting) and the Colleagues of Calligraphy. When she's not holding a writing tool, she's likely to be exploring the trails and shorelines of Duluth, Minnesota, with family and friends, reading, or trying to keep the pantry stocked for hungry teenagers. Check out more of her work on *Instagram* @calligraphybybrenna or her website: BrennaJordan.com.